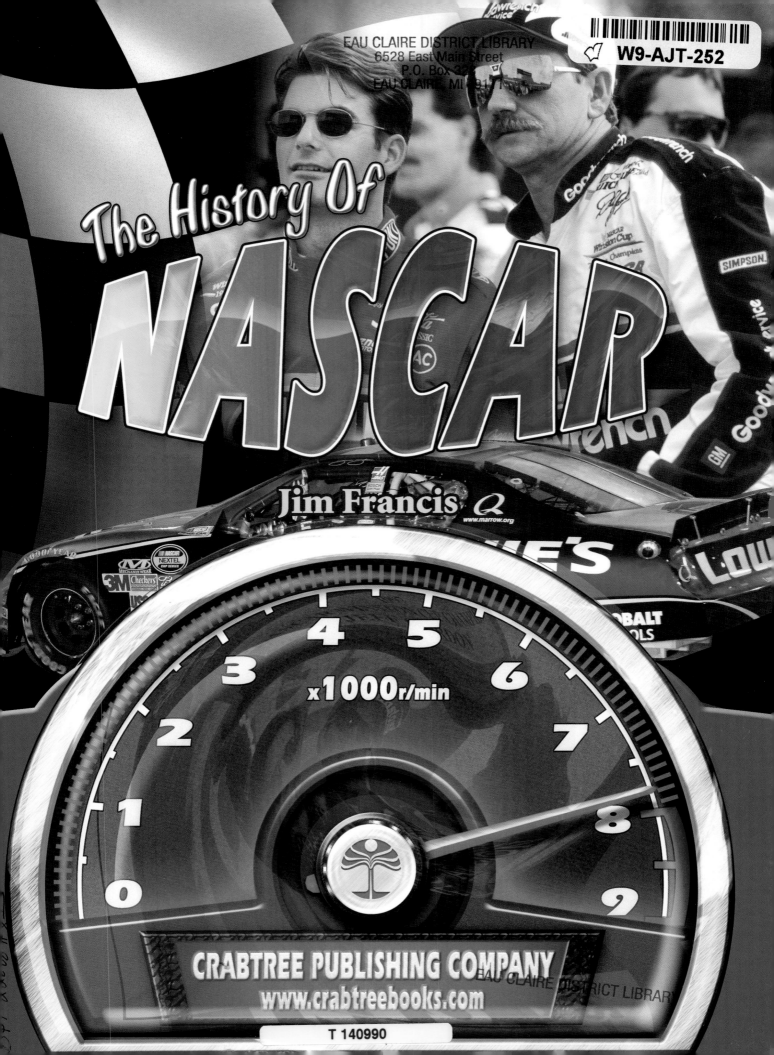

The History Of NASCAR

Jim Francis

x1000r/min

CRABTREE PUBLISHING COMPANY
www.crabtreebooks.com

Crabtree Publishing Company

www.crabtreebooks.com

Coordinating editor
Chester Fisher

Series and project editor
Shoreline Publishing Group LLC

Author
Jim Francis

Project Manager
Kavita Lad (Q2AMEDIA)

Art direction
Rahul Dhiman (Q2AMEDIA)

Design
Tarang Saggar (Q2AMEDIA)

Cover Design
Dalbir Singh (Q2AMEDIA)

Photo research
Anasuya Acharya & Amit Tigga (Q2AMEDIA)

Manuscript development and photo research
assistance provided by Shoreline Publishing
Group LLC, Santa Barbara, California

Acknowledgments

The publishers would like to thanks the following for permission
to reproduce photographs:

AP Photo: pages 8, 9, 11, 12, 15, 17 (top); Ric Feld:
    page 17 (bottom); James P. Kerlin: page 7 (top);
    Jim Kerlin: page 13; Chris O'Meara: page 20;
    Lynne Sladky: cover; Pete Wright: page 6
Lowe's Motor Speedway Archives/Nascar Media: pages 19,
    21 (bottom)
Motorsports Images & Archives/Nascar Media: page 18
Nascar Media: pages 10, 15 (top), 16, 21 (top)
Joe Robbins: title page, pages 5, 14, 22, 23, 24, 25, 26, 27,
    28, 29, 31
Grey Villet/Time Life Pictures/Getty Image: pages 4, 7 (bottom)

Cover: Richard Petty of Randleman, N.C., walks down
pit row before the start of the 125 mile Daytona 500
qualifying race Thursday afternoon Feb. 14, 1992 at
Daytona International Speedway.

Title page: (top) Dale Earnhardt alongside Jeff Gordon in 1995.
(bottom) Jimmie Johnson celebrates 2006 Nextel Cup
Championship

Library and Archives Canada Cataloguing in Publication

Francis, Jim, 1963-
    The history of NASCAR / Jim Francis.

(NASCAR)
Includes index.
ISBN 978-0-7787-3186-3 (bound).--ISBN 978-0-7787-3194-8 (pbk.)

    1. NASCAR (Association)--History--Juvenile literature. 2. Stock
car racing--United States--History--Juvenile literature. 3. Stock cars
(Automobiles)--Juvenile literature. I. Title. II. Series: NASCAR
(St. Catharines, Ont.)

GV1029.9.S74F73 2007   j796.72   C2007-907258-5

Library of Congress Cataloging-in-Publication Data

Francis, Jim, 1963-
  The history of NASCAR / Jim Francis.
    p. cm.
  Includes index.
  ISBN-13: 978-0-7787-3186-3 (rlb)
  ISBN-10: 0-7787-3186-3 (rlb)
  ISBN-13: 978-0-7787-3194-8 (pb)
  ISBN-10: 0-7787-3194-4 (pb)
  1. Stock car racing--United States--History--Juvenile literature. 2. NASCAR
(Association)--History--Juvenile literature. I. Title.
  GV1029.9.S74F726 2008
  796.720973--dc22
                 2007048439

Crabtree Publishing Company

www.crabtreebooks.com   1-800-387-7650

Published in Canada
Crabtree Publishing
616 Welland Ave.
St. Catharines, ON
L2M 5V6

Published in the United States
Crabtree Publishing
PMB16A
350 Fifth Ave., Suite 3308
New York, NY 10118

Published in the United Kingdom
Crabtree Publishing
White Cross Mills
High Town, Lancaster
LA1 4XS

Published in Australia
Crabtree Publishing
386 Mt. Alexander Rd.
Ascot Vale (Melbourne)
VIC 3032

CONTENTS

NASCAR Today....
and Yesterday

NASCAR has gone from racing big, rumbling **stock cars** on dusty tracks in the South to thrilling millions with high-tech racing on enormous superspeedways.

Start Your Engines!

Powerful engines drown out the roar of the crowd as the NASCAR race is about to start. Every seat is filled in the gigantic track, as fans wait for the 43 high-tech cars to reach top speed. The green flag drops and the race is on! The drivers steer their mighty machines inches away from other cars, battling for top position. The action will continue for hours, thrilling millions watching on TV and hundreds of thousands watching in person. This is NASCAR today.

NASCAR, which stands for National Association for Stock Car Auto Racing, has come a long way from its humble beginnings in the American South. Early racers were simply the guys with the fastest cars in their home garages.

Big cars, fast drivers: Here's dusty action from a NASCAR race in 1958.

4

*Today's NASCAR racers, like Jeff Gordon (right),
steer high-tech machines around enormous tracks in front of huge crowds.*

They raced for fun on weekends in front of small crowds of fellow "car nuts." However, once the drivers got organized in 1948, they began a building process that has made NASCAR America's most popular and most exciting motor sport.

NASCAR Zooms Ahead

NASCAR's growth, as we'll see, was slow and steady . . . until the last decade or so. After its start in the South in the late 1940s, the sport quickly caught on with a large audience in the Southern states. Today, this part of the country remains the area that still gives NASCAR its biggest support—and many of its most famous drivers. However, in the 1970s, new interest from **sponsors** and TV audiences sent interest soaring

nationally. And in the 1990s, that interest rocketed upward almost faster than its cars zoom around the track. Today's drivers can earn many millions of dollars, compared to the low thousands that early drivers took home. NASCAR drivers today appear in national commercials, have dozens of sponsors, write best-selling books, and even appear in movies. Like a long and hard-fought race, NASCAR's race to the top of the American sports scene had many stops and starts, high points and low points. But everyone who has been a part of that ride, on or off the track, has had a great time— because they all shared the need for speed! Strap on your helmet, and let's go along for the ride as NASCAR powers up.

Big Bill's Big Dream

NASCAR owes much of its success to the dream of one man who helped guide the sport from rough-and-tumble beginnings to national acceptance.

Big Bill France, shown here later in life, began as a stock car driver in 1930s Florida.

The Chase Is On!

The roots of stock car racing start on dusty back roads in the Deep South—with a little help from some outlaws. In the 1920s and 1930s, making and selling alcohol was illegal. Many people in the South made something called "moonshine," which was a type of liquor. To avoid the police, the moonshiners put their product in fast cars and found heavy-footed men who loved to drive fast! The chases between moonshiners and the law inspired some of the drivers to take their cars to the track and race.

In these pre-NASCAR races, drivers often just steered their family cars onto rough dirt tracks. They drove without helmets, seat belts, or other safety gear. Instead of the giant pit crews of today's NASCAR, in those days, a driver might get out to change his own tires, or just get a pal to help out on race day. The track owners decided when the races would be held and how much the drivers could earn—which usually wasn't very much. Drivers held little power or control over their racing lives off the track.

Sand-churning, high-flying action from Daytona Beach in the 1940s.

On the Beach

Meanwhile, other drivers were using the hard-packed sands of Daytona Beach, Florida, to race their own souped-up hot rods. The beach course would take the drivers roaring down the sand. They would then pull into tight turns and churn through soft sand, often only a few feet from a crowd of spectators. After a lap on a city street, the course took them back onto the hard beach. Round and round they went on this famous course, sometimes rolling their cars in spectacular, sand-churning crashes. These drivers loved racing as much as their moonshine-running cousins, who also raced on dirt tracks throughout the South. Together, these two groups would come together to form NASCAR.

Packed stands and fast racers were a dream come true for Bill France.

Two-time champ Herb Thomas (left) along with Fireball Roberts and Curtis Turner.

Big Bill Creates NASCAR

One of the drivers from Daytona Beach was a tall, lanky fellow who went by the name of "Big" Bill France. He had been a driver for more than 10 years. Like many drivers, he felt that the people putting on the races were not being fair to the drivers who risked their lives for very little money. Plus, with races held at tracks all over the South, there was no way to know who was the best overall driver. By the 1940s, France and other drivers wanted a more organized way to race. In late 1947, they met in Daytona Beach, Florida, to form a new group. They called it the National Association for Stock Car Auto Racing, and France was chosen as the first president. The group set up a series of races beginning in 1949. The drivers would earn points from each of the races, depending on how they finished. The driver with most points at the end of the season would be named the "Grand National" champion.

Early NASCAR Stars

While France battled with track owners for fair treatment, drivers battled on the tracks for victories. Red Byron and Bob Flock emerged as top drivers, with each winning two races in that first year. Byron ended up the season champion.

Bill Rexford was indeed No. 1—he was the 1950 NASCAR Grand National champion.

8

Other names from early NASCAR became legends thanks to their hard-charging, winning styles. Lee Petty won one race during that first season, the first of 54 that he won in his career. That was the all-time best until his son, Richard, came along to break the mark. Lee was also the first driver to win three Grand National season championships. Glenn "Fireball" Roberts and Curtis Turner became winners and folk heroes. Bob Flock's entire family played a big part in NASCAR. Tim Flock won two season championships—and drove eight races in 1953 with a monkey as his co-pilot. Jocko Flocko didn't do anything but ride along, but the fuzzy passenger remains a great NASCAR story. Bob and Tim's brother Fonty, as well as their sister Ethel, also drove in some races.

Part of the popularity of NASCAR stemmed from fans like these who liked to race their own cars on the beach in Florida.

NASCAR Firsts

In any sport, it's good to know who was the "first" in various areas. Here are some cool NASCAR firsts:

- **First Grand National Race:** At Charlotte, North Carolina, June 19, 1949
- **First Official Race Winner:** Jim Roper, driving a 1949 Lincoln
- **First Winner on a Daytona Track:** Red Byron, July 10, 1949
- **First NASCAR Champion:** Red Byron, 1949
- **First Driver with Four Race Wins in a Season:** Curtis Turner, 1950
- **First Driver to Win Two NASCAR Championships:** Herb Thomas, 1951 and 1953

Birth of Daytona

The next big step forward for NASCAR was the creation of newer and bigger tracks. At places like Daytona International Speedway, the sport roared into the future.

Big Bill (left) with Big Bill Jr., who would take over NASCAR from his dad.

Here Comes the Speedway

In 1950, Darlington Raceway opened for business. At 1.25 miles (2 km), it was the longest speedway in the country at the time. It was also paved with asphalt. The first race there was the Southern 500, and Johnny Mantz won it at an average speed of 76 miles per hour (122 km/h). The new track inspired the building of other new tracks that were even longer. The new tracks also featured higher **banking** in the turns. This meant that the roadway was tilted in all four corners of the oval course. This banking helped the drivers keep up their speed through the turns. With these new tracks, NASCAR itself sped up in popularity, too.

More Champions

Throughout the 1950s, more and more top drivers emerged to challenge for the Grand National title. In 1956 and 1957, Buddy Baker won the top trophy; he won 24 races over the two seasons. Junior Johnson, a former moonshine runner, was near the top in several seasons. He would go on to become one of the sport's most successful car owners. His drivers won several national titles. Glenn "Fireball" Roberts was among the top drivers, too, along with a driver with another great nickname, "Speedy" Thompson.

The First 500

In 1959, NASCAR's biggest track yet opened up and soon became the sport's centerpiece site. Daytona International Speedway was 2.5 miles (4 km) around and had room for more than 150,000 fans. The first major race held there was the Daytona 500, which is still the most important race of the season today. The 1959 Daytona 500 featured a triple photo-finish. Three cars, two of them on the lead lap, finished at almost the same instant. Johnny Beauchamp was declared the winner, but days later, close-up photos showed that Lee Petty had come in first. The close race gave NASCAR some of its first national attention. All that news coverage, along with the crowds at the new tracks, brought in more companies hoping to sell cars. NASCAR was growing up fast..

Meanwhile, the sport's signature race grew rapidly, too. By the middle of the 1960s, it was known as "The Great American Race." Even today, the Daytona 500 in mid-February kicks off every NASCAR season and draws the biggest crowds and highest television ratings. Richard Petty holds the record for most Daytona 500 wins with seven. Jeff Gordon was the youngest winner at 23 years old in 1995.

Lee Petty (car 42 below, and right) edged out Johnny Beauchamp to win the 1959 Daytona 500.

Here Comes The King

NASCAR needed a national hero to help spread the sport beyond the South. During the decade of the 1960s, one driver emerged to fill that role: Richard Petty.

Lee's Little Boy

Though NASCAR was 10 years old, it was still stuck in the Deep South. Most races were held there, and more fans lived in that region than anywhere else. The races didn't usually get national coverage. But that all changed thanks to Richard Petty. The son of three-time champ Lee Petty, Richard grew up following his dad to races. He worked on Lee's **pit crew** and back home in the garage. NASCAR was in his blood, and he was itching to race. However, Lee made Richard wait until he was 21 before letting him join the big boys on the track. Richard made up for lost time by winning **rookie** of the year honors in 1959. He won his first race in 1960—the first of many. By the time he retired in 1984, Richard Petty had won 200 races, nearly twice as many as the second-highest driver. He would start more races, win more **pole positions**, and finish in more top 10s and with more NASCAR championships than any other driver. In all, Petty would end up holding 15 important NASCAR career records, including most races started at 1,177. He would become a legend. By 1964, however, Lee's boy Richard had won his first NASCAR championship. But he was just getting started.

A young King: Petty was the 1959 NASCAR rookie of the year.

The King is Born

In 1967, Petty put together one of the greatest single seasons of success in American sports history. He won an incredible 27 of the 48 races that he entered that year, including a record 10 in a row. He missed finishing in the top five in only 10 races all year long. In May, he broke his dad's all-time career record by capturing his 55th race win. He won twice as much money as the second-place finisher on the season, while capturing 19 pole positions. Along with his second of a

record seven NASCAR titles, that year Petty earned his famous nickname: The King. Petty continued to dominate NASCAR for more than a decade, winning championships in 1971, 1972, 1974, 1975, and 1979. Only the great Dale Earnhardt Sr. has matched Petty's seven titles in the decades since. Along the way, Petty won seven Daytona 500 championships, another all-time record. He won his 200th victory in the 1984 Firecracker 500 at Daytona International Speedway (other races are held at Daytona besides the 500). President Ronald Reagan was in attendance at the July 4 event, the first time a U.S. president had been to a NASCAR race. It was another sign of NASCAR's growth on the American sports scene.

One of 200: Petty filled a museum with his race trophies.

The Big Time

Another sign of how things were improving for drivers was the ever-growing amounts of money that they were earning. For example, Petty's total winnings in 1967, his most successful season in terms of race victories, were about $130,000. By the time he won his seventh title in 1979, he was earning more than $500,000 per year. Those dollar figures would keep rising in the years ahead. Led by increases in sponsorship and in money from TV **contracts**, the very best NASCAR drivers were earning nearly a million dollars a year by the 1980s. However, for fans, it still came down to wins and heroes, not dollars and cents. They loved the drivers, and followed them like members of the family. The career and stunning victory totals of Petty—along with his smiling personality—gave the NASCAR family its first true national hero.

The King's Championships

Year	Race Wins	Points*
1964	9	40,252
1967	27	42,272
1971	21	4,435
1972	8	8,701
1974	10	5,037
1975	13	4,783
1979	5	4,830

*The way points were calculated changed over the years, so annual numbers don't always match up.

Petty's No. 1 Rival

Every great champion needs a rival, and for Richard Petty, that rival was David Pearson. The man they called "The Silver Fox" won 105 total races, second only to The King. The two ace drivers finished first and second in 63 races, with Pearson winning 33 of those head-to-head battles. Pearson also won three NASCAR championships, in 1966, 1968, and 1969. The most famous of those battles took place in the 1976 Daytona 500. As the two drivers entered the final turn, both had a shot at the checkered flag. First one, then the other, inched ahead. Then suddenly, they collided, swerved into the outer wall, and slid back down to the grass on the inside of the track. Pearson managed to restart his battered car and inched across the finish line moments later. Petty was stuck in the grass, his car smoking.

Cale Takes Three Straight

In the mid-1970s, a hard-driving South Carolina native put the brakes to Richard Petty's dominance. Cale Yarborough was the NASCAR champion in 1976, 1977, and 1978—he remains the only driver to win three straight titles. He also finished second in the season standings in three other seasons, and his 83 race victories are fifth all-time. Cale loved racing at Daytona International Speedway especially. His four titles at the famed Daytona 500 are the second-most of all-time, trailing—who else?—Richard Petty, who had seven wins in that race.

David Pearson (No. 3) was a three-time NASCAR champ and Petty's chief rival.

By the 1970s, NASCAR had gone national, as at this race in Ontario, California.

Big Bill Jr. Takes Over

While Petty, Pearson, Yarborough, and other drivers helped NASCAR race ahead in the 1970s, there was a big change off the track. Big Bill France Sr. had run NASCAR since its first race in 1949. No one had more impact on making NASCAR grow than Big Bill,

but he retired in 1972. Taking over was his son, Bill Jr. Young Bill had grown up around the sport, and had learned at his father's side how to deal with drivers, track owners, carmakers, and many others. Bill Jr., however, had a new group of people that he had to work with. In the 1970s, more and more NASCAR races were being shown, at least in part, on TV. Bill Jr. worked hard to make sure that new contracts for televising races were signed, for more and more money.

The Successor: Bill France Jr. carried on the family business in 1972, leading NASCAR for more than 30 years.

Here Comes the Money!

While NASCAR drivers drove for the love of speed, they also wanted to earn a living. By the 1970s, sponsors and TV money had turned NASCAR into a bigtime sport.

NASCAR Winston Cup Series

Thanks to money from cigarette maker Winston, NASCAR could afford to reach millions more fans around the country.

Winston Comes On Board

One of the biggest things leading to more TV money was more sponsorship money. In 1972, NASCAR made its biggest change off the track yet. A major American cigarette company signed on to provide millions of dollars of prize money and promotional support for NASCAR. In return, the annual championship was changed from the Grand National to the Winston Cup. Winston got tons of advertising, as newspaper articles and TV sports shows all now discussed the battle for the Winston Cup. To the drivers, it meant increased prize money. The exposure of being on TV more often also brought in other sponsors. Richard Petty's deal in 1972 with STP was the most famous. STP made engine treatment products; its logo was all over Petty's famous No. 43 car for the rest of his career. Other drivers found ways to get many sponsors' names stuck to their cars. For the most part, each driver or race team signed up their own sponsors. In many cases, they were companies with local ties to the drivers' hometowns or sold products that appealed to that drivers' fans. NASCAR also signed up national sponsors to appear on all cars, starting with Winston, but including tire, gasoline, and automobile companies.

A Fight Makes Great TV

Oddly, the event that gained the most attention for NASCAR in this period was not a race or a championship—but a fight! In 1979, the Daytona 500 was televised live from start to finish and nationwide for the first time. An enormous audience saw Richard Petty win the race, but that was not the big story. Petty actually won the race after Cale Yarborough and Donnie Allison got into a last-lap crash. Following the race, the two, joined by Allison's brother Bobby, got into a fistfight on the infield after climbing out of their cars. Fans on TV watched in amazement as the trio punched and kicked at each other. No one was hurt in the fight or the crashes, but the action led to lots more coverage of NASCAR races.

This 1979 crash between Cale Yarborough (No. 11) and Donnie Allison (No. 1) led to the battle shown below—and to increased national attention for NASCAR.

Bobby Allison has Cale Yarborough in a foot-lock, while Bobby's brother Donnie tries to get at Cale with his helmet!

The 1980s Speed Up

With TV and sponsor money starting to increase, drivers got faster and faster cars . . . and a new NASCAR legend emerged to take the place of "The King".

Slowing Things Down?

NASCAR drivers always aimed for going as fast as they could. But in the 1980s, improvement in engines and cars made them go too fast. On the larger superspeedways, race speeds were getting too high, officials felt, and endangering drivers. In 1987, Bill Elliott set a new record by steering his Ford more than 212 miles (341 km) per hour during a qualifying lap. For the safety of the drivers and spectators, NASCAR decided to slow things down at the superspeedways. For all races on longer tracks, drivers had to install a "restrictor plate" in their engines. This square piece of metal would lower the amount of air that got into the engines. This reduced the power of the engines and the speed of the car. Off the track, NASCAR and its popularity kept going up and up.

Bill Elliott (shown here driving a different car) set a new speed record in a Ford Thunderbird at Talladega.

Another Champion Son

The most successful and popular driver of the 1980s—and most of the 1990s—was another Southern native and son of a former NASCAR driver. Dale Earnhardt Sr. followed in the high-speed footsteps of his father Ralph, who had raced in the 1950s. Dale Sr. won his first NASCAR title in his second full season, 1980. Earnhardt became a fan favorite for his quiet determination. He wasn't flashy—he seemed like one of the boys around the garage. In 1986, he won his second title while driving the No. 3 car for the first time. His new sponsor, the Goodwrench repair company, gave the car a black paint job, and Earnhardt put on a black helmet. He became "The Man in Black." He also became well-known for his ability to bump, nudge, or jar opponents during a race, pushing them aside to help him win. From this technique, he earned another nickname: "The **Intimidator**."

Dale Earnhardt Sr. is the only man other than Petty with seven NASCAR titles.

The 1986 season was the start of one of the most dominant periods in NASCAR history. From 1986 to 1994, Earnhardt finished first six times and finished in the top three in two other seasons.

Busch Begins

In 1982, NASCAR created another series of races. Well, not really created—just renamed and improved. Since 1950, slightly slower stock cars had raced in a series called the "Late Model Sportsman." In 1982, however, this second group of races got a new sponsor, a bigger schedule, and more attention. It was sponsored by a beer company and called the Busch Series. The series, now sort of a minor league of NASCAR and called the Nationwide Series beginning in 2008, has an annual champion and runs about 35 races a year.

Money, Money!

Though Dale Earnhardt Sr. was the dominant racer in the 1980s and early 1990s, other drivers were emerging as stars. Darrell Waltrip won the title in 1981, 1982, and 1985. His car was owned by Junior Johnson, the former NASCAR driver and moonshine runner. Johnson's success (he also owned Cale Yarborough's car) was a great link for fans to NASCAR's dirt-road past. Bobby Allison won in 1983, watched by Donnie, his brother and fellow driver. In 1984, Terry Labonte continued the family theme. When his brother Bobby won in 2000, they became the first brothers to each capture the title. More importantly for Terry, however, his 1984 title marked the first time that a NASCAR champ earned more than $1 million in a season.

Darrell Waltrip shows how drivers get into their NASCAR rides—through a window opening.

Million Dollar Bill

While Dale Earnhardt Sr. won more championships, Bill Elliott won just as many hearts. In annual voting among fans for the Most Popular Driver, Elliott won that honor an amazing 16 times. He began his driving career in 1977, driving for his father's team. His brother Ernie was the chief mechanic. Elliott quickly got a reputation as a guy who liked high speeds. Remember, he would go on to set an all-time speed record in 1987. In 1985, however, at the height of his fame, he did something that no other driver had done. By winning the Daytona 500, the Winston 500, and the Southern 500 in the same year, he won a special $1 million prize. And with it, got his most famous nickname: "Million Dollar Bill." Elliott won his only NASCAR title two years later and continued racing regularly until the early 2000s, remaining among the sport's most popular athletes.

Rusty Wallace was one of three trios of brothers to earn rides at NASCAR's highest level, continuing the sport's long family tradition.

NASCAR Families

Since its earliest days, families racing together has been a part of NASCAR. Here's a chart of some of the more notable racing clans:

Fathers and Sons

Bobby*, Davey, and Clifford Allison

Buck* and Buddy Baker

Dale* and Dale Earnhardt

Ned* and Dale Jarrett*

Lee* and Richard Petty*

Richard*, Kyle, and Adam Petty

*NASCAR champion

Brothers

Bobby* and Donnie Allison

Geoff, Brett, and Todd Bodine

Kurt* and Kyle Busch

Jeff and Ward Burton

Tim*, Fonty, and Bob Flock
   (and sister Ethel)

Terry* and Bobby* Labonte

Darrell* and Michael Waltrip

Rusty*, Mike, and Kenny Wallace.

Rusty Wallace (27), here battling Darrell Waltrip, was the 1989 champ.

Close Races and New Stars

As Richard Petty said goodbye in 1992, new stars like Jeff Gordon emerged to keep NASCAR's rocket ride upward going stronger—and faster—than ever.

A Race to the Finish

In 1992, NASCAR saw its closest championship finish to date. Going into the final race, Donnie Allison held a 30-point lead in the season standings. Bill Elliott and Alan Kulwicki were close, but needed help. They got it late in the final race in Atlanta, when Allison crashed. Kulwicki and Elliott raced in first and second place for the final laps, with each lap they led adding points to their total. The final result came down to Kulwicki leading 103 laps to Elliott's 102. The five-point bonus was enough to clinch Kulwicki's victory. The result also marked the end of an era in NASCAR. Kulwicki was the last driver to win a title in a car that he owned. The growth of the sport meant that it took much more money and time than any one person had to keep a car on the track. Car owners were now

In 1992, Alan Kulwicki (right, battling No. 43 Richard Petty) was the last owner-driver to win the NASCAR championship.

large businesses, employing hundreds of people. The technology of the cars meant that it cost millions just to keep it running. But the gritty Kulwicki won one more for the "old school." Earnhardt, meanwhile, got his revenge, winning his seventh and final title in 1994, matching the great Richard Petty for most all-time title wins. Other top drivers of the 1990s included Dale Jarrett, whose father Ned, was the 1961 and 1965 NASCAR champ; Mark Martin, a popular driver with three second-place season finishes; and Rusty Wallace, the 1989 champion. Meanwhile, Richard "The King" Petty retired in 1992 after a season-long farewell tour.

The Kid Is a Champ

The mid-1990s saw the birth of a new NASCAR legend. Jeff Gordon had grown up in California racing go-karts. His family moved to Indiana when he was nine. Jeff fell in love with the **open-wheel** racers that roared around the famous Indianapolis Motor Speedway. He won several national titles in sports cars, with an eye toward driving Indy cars one day. However, after his first ride in a stock car when he was 19, he was hooked. He started out in the Busch Series and was an instant success, winning 11 races in 1991. He made his first NASCAR start in 1992 in Richard Petty's last race. In 1993, Gordon reached NASCAR's top level to stay. The following year, Jeff's Indy dream came true. For the first time, a NASCAR race was held at Indy, one of the world's most famous tracks. And the kid who grew up watching races there won the first Brickyard 500. (The Brickyard is a nickname for the Indy track, which used to be paved in bricks.) Gordon kept his amazing young career going by winning his first NASCAR championship in 1995. At only 24, he was the youngest champ of the modern era, which NASCAR counts as beginning in 1972. To win that first title, Gordon had to beat out the legendary Dale Earnhardt by 34 points. Gordon won seven races that year and captured eight pole positions, while setting a new single-season earnings record. Between race winnings and year-end bonuses, he earned more than $4.3 million! But it would not be the last time that "The Kid" stood atop the NASCAR rankings.

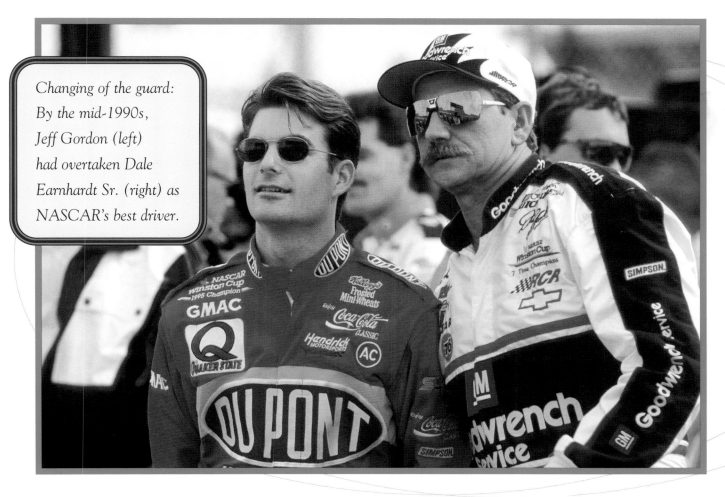

Changing of the guard: By the mid-1990s, Jeff Gordon (left) had overtaken Dale Earnhardt Sr. (right) as NASCAR's best driver.

NASCAR Races to the Future

As Jeff Gordon became the new face of NASCAR, a new TV deal helped the sport rocket upward in popularity. But a tragedy marred NASCAR's enormous growth.

New Tracks, New Fans

The late 1990s were a great time to be a NASCAR fan. Every race was on TV, so millions more fans could enjoy the action. New tracks were built in places like Texas, Las Vegas, Miami, and Los Angeles, far from the tracks' Southern roots. A new web site brought instant news of race results to fans around the world. And a

new rivalry brought lots of attention to the racing action. Following his championship in 1995, Jeff Gordon was the new face of NASCAR. His fresh, young image contrasted with the gruff "good ol' boy" look of Dale Earnhardt Sr. and others. Dale's fans hated Gordon, while Gordon's fans thought Dale was a bit old-fashioned. For his part, Earnhardt knew that Gordon was good, but he wasn't ready to give up his crown so easily. He even suggested that Gordon "drink some milk" to celebrate the '95 title! Their rivalry on the track continued to be a hot topic in NASCAR for the next several years. Gordon got the best of it, however, winning two more titles, in 1997 and 1998, and outdueling Earnhardt to win the Daytona 500 in 1999. Earnhardt was right on Gordon's rear bumper for the final laps, "the longest 10 laps of my life," said Gordon afterward.

Passing the Torch
With his second overall title in 1997, Jeff Gordon showed that the "The Kid" was ready to take over as the face of NASCAR, leaving many older drivers in his wake.

24

Dale's Big Day

While Gordon was winning titles, Earnhardt still knew how to win hearts. In 19 previous tries, Earnhardt had never won the famed Daytona 500, though he had won more than 30 other events at the Daytona International Speedway. He had come very close on several occasions, only to fall short. One time he ran out of gas, another time he blew a tire, while a third time he got involved in a late-race wreck. The greatest victory race **eluded** the greatest driver. Finally, in 1998, he left all of his challengers and bad breaks behind. For the first time in his amazing 20-year career, Earnhardt Sr. was the Daytona 500 champion. A line of crew members from all of his opponents lined **pit road** to congratulate him. Even his fellow drivers said they were happy for the Man in Black. He stuck with it and finally won at Daytona.

Dream Come True
In 1998, racing fans everywhere joined Dale Earnhardt Sr. when he celebrated—finally!— his first victory in the legendary Daytona 500.

Race Trucks, Not Cars

NASCAR is not just about racecars. Beginning in 1995, they started racing pickup trucks, too, in the NASCAR Craftsman Truck Series. The trucks are specially modified for racing, including enclosing the back and souping up the engines. Most of the races are run on the same tracks as NASCAR events, often on the same weekends. Several former truck-series drivers went on to success in cars at the top level, such as Greg Biffle, Kurt Busch, and Todd Bodine. Jack Sprague won the most season titles with three (1997, 1999, 2001), while Ron Hornaday Jr.'s 29 race wins are the most of all-time.

Big TV News

As the 2000s neared, NASCAR saw a chance to make a huge leap forward. They matched TV networks and cable channels against each other, looking for the best deal. What they got was light years away from what Big Bill France Sr. could ever have imagined 50 years earlier way down South. In late 1999, NASCAR signed a deal with several TV networks that would pay the racing group $2.4 billion. Billion, with a "B"! It was one of the largest TV **contracts** ever signed and immediately meant that NASCAR would be on TV more often, and in more places, than ever before. This meant more time for sponsors to get their messages on TV, more money for driver earnings, and more money to spend on technology. The TV contract pushed NASCAR forward faster than any previous event.

You're On!
Drivers like Jimmie Johnson and sponsors like Lowe's know the importance of getting airtime from the many TV cameras at NASCAR races.

Tragedy Touches NASCAR

Though the TV contract, which started with the 2001 season, was great news, the new century also started on a sad note for NASCAR. Racecar drivers know that their sport can be a dangerous one. High speeds and close racing mean that almost every race has at least one wreck. There have been many injuries and some deaths in the past. But this death hit perhaps hardest of all. Just before the end of the 2001 Daytona 500, Dale Earnhardt Sr. was bumped, spun, and slammed into the wall. He was killed instantly. Millions mourned his death, and many still do. He remains one of the sport's most popular drivers, and you can't go to a race without seeing a black No. 3 displayed somewhere. The only bright spot to this tragedy was that NASCAR made many safety improvements, to both cars and tracks, that might one day save other drivers' lives.

A Sad Day
Dale Earnhardt Jr. (in red) was one of millions who mourned the loss in 2001 of his father, one of NASCAR's greatest drivers.

Another France Takes Over

Most sports in America are run by team owners or by an organization that has many members. NASCAR is run—as it has been from the start—by one family. Though the sport is now a billion-dollar, international sports giant, the Frances are still in charge. In 2003, Brian France, the latest in line, took over from his father and grandfather. Brian, like his dad Bill Jr., had grown up in NASCAR. He had known from an early age that he might be in charge one day. He studied business, technology and **marketing**—the sorts of things that a modern sports leader needs to know about. He was not a racer, he was a boss. Under Brian, NASCAR has made some big changes. The biggest was the new sponsorship of Nextel (later Sprint) and the creation of the **Chase for the Cup** (see box on page 30). Brian also signed new TV agreements that expanded the already-huge contract. More so than the previous Frances who had run the sport, Brian knows that he needs lots of experts around him to help run NASCAR. But as has been true since 1948, a France is still in charge.

(see box on page 30)

France Family Legacy

No family has had a bigger hold on an American sport than the Frances. This chart shows the years that they each ran NASCAR.

Bill France Sr. — 1948-1972
Bill France Jr. — 1972-2003
Brian France — 2003-present

Brian France is the third member of his family to run the mighty motor-sports empire.

Filled Up
Fans pack superspeedways like Talladega in Alabama to watch their heroes go for the checkered flag.

NASCAR Aims for the World

With its millions of fans in America happy, NASCAR looks to the world to help grow its sport.

Let's Get Bigger!

Taking advantage of the growing interest in NASCAR, the series organizers looked to spread news of their sport to new places. The annual awards banquet had been in New York City since 1980. But the new exposure of the big TV contract sent NASCAR back to the drawing board. The event was built up into a bigger deal, put on TV, and promoted much more often. Great photos of NASCAR racing machines lined up in famous Times Square and champs posing with the trophy in Central Park attracted new attention for NASCAR. The NASCAR.com website was much improved, and now offered fans tons of video and audio clips. For the first time, they could listen in on radio conversations between drivers and crews. The big names like Gordon and Dale Earnhardt Jr. found themselves treated like celebrities on TV talk shows and even in movies. Dale Jr.'s autobiography, *Driver #8*, was a bestseller in 2002.

Winner!
Jimmie Johnson, the 2006 NASCAR champ, waves his hand on a victory lap during a 2006 race.

International NASCAR

Meanwhile, NASCAR was not content with just winning fans in the United States. In 2005, a Busch Series race was held in Mexico for the first time. A 2007 Busch race took place outside Montreal, Canada. Also in 2007, Spanish native Juan Pablo Montoya joined NASCAR. The former **Formula 1** racing star became the first foreign-born race winner since 1974 when he captured the 2007 Toyota Save Mart 300. Another Formula 1 star, Frenchman Jacques Villeneuve, announced that he would drive in NASCAR truck races in 2008. Veteran Champ Car series driver (Indy-style open-wheel cars) A. J. Allmendinger has switched to stock cars full-time. And the biggest international news for NASCAR came in 2007, when Japanese carmaker Toyota became the first foreign company to make cars that run in NASCAR's car series (it had earlier supplied some trucks for Craftsman races).

Next Wave
Former Formula 1 driver Juan-Pablo Montoya is one of several foreign drivers drawn to the money and fame of NASCAR.

The Big Time!
NASCAR's 2005 champion, Tony Stewart, posed in New York City's Times Square with the shiny new Nextel Cup.

New Sponsor, New Name, New Fans

From 1972 to 2003, the NASCAR champion won the Winston Cup. In 2004, however, that changed with the addition of a new top sponsor. Thanks to a giant telephone company, the top trophy is now called the Sprint Cup (it was the Nextel Cup from 2004-2007). Since NASCAR was no longer connected to a cigarette company, many more national ad programs could be created. Until then, children's products were not often connected with NASCAR to avoid promoting cigarette use among kids. However, with a telephone company as the main sponsor, advertising to kids about NASCAR shot up. A new generation of fans found it easier and more fun to follow NASCAR. One driver even got his car sponsored by M&Ms candy, while numerous new books and video games were put out to help young fans learn about the sport and their favorite drivers.

The Car of Tomorrow . . . Today

Beginning in 2008, all NASCAR teams will use the same basic car shape. Created after years of testing, the cars include new safety features that will help protect drivers. Plus, having the same car means that the races will be greater tests of racing skill, as opposed to battles between mechanics. The biggest change in the look of the car is a "spoiler" bar on the back to help drivers keep control at high speeds. Teams can adjust that bar, and a similar part up front, to match the needs of the track and each individual driver. Another goal of the new car is to try to make the races contests of driving skill, not necessarily great engine or car building. From Cars of Tomorrow to giant TV contracts, from international drivers to ever-growing numbers of fans, NASCAR continues to grow. Like the races that its fans love, NASCAR is moving forward, and they're getting there fast!

Chase for the Cup

Until 2004, NASCAR champions were determined by points earned during all races in the season. Whoever ended up with the most points won. In 2004, however, a new system was begun to create a type of playoffs to encourage more fan interest. Now, during the first 26 races, drivers earn points for wins, laps led, and other things. After the first 26 races, the top 12 drivers qualify for a special "Chase for the Cup." Their points are reset so that only a few points separate the top 12. During the season's final 10 races, these 12 drivers try to earn enough points to end up in the top spot and win what is now called the Sprint Cup. Once the Chase begins, no driver but one of those top 12 can become the champ.

Track Types

NASCAR's first tracks were all-dirt ovals, usually not more than a half-mile long. In today's NASCAR, races are run on four types of tracks, all of which have an asphalt or concrete road surface

Superspeedway: at least 2 miles (3.2 km) long, usually an oval with banked corners; some are D-shaped instead of oval.

Speedway: at least 1 mile (1.6 km) long with banks in the turns

Short-track: one-half to 1 mile (0.8 to 1.6 km) long, with tighter turns and higher banking

Road: a twisting layout with many turns instead of just four. The surface is flat, with no banks, and calls for much more braking and steering than the other tracks do

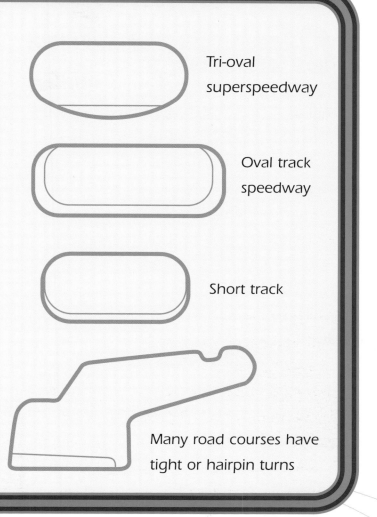

Tri-oval superspeedway

Oval track speedway

Short track

Many road courses have tight or hairpin turns

The Chase continues for NASCAR, led by 2006 and 2007 Cup champion Jimmie Johnson (48).

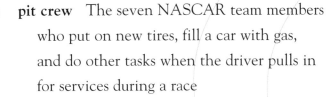

Glossary

banking   The steeply angled corners of racetracks that let cars maintain higher speeds, even while making turns

contracts   Agreements between people or companies written down and signed to make sure that everyone agrees on the terms

eluded   Escaped from

Formula 1   A popular, international, open-wheel racing circuit

intimidator   A person who threatens others by his or her personality

marketing   Using advertising and other ways to convince people to buy a product or service

open-wheel   A type of racecar that has a tube-shaped body and no fenders over the tires

pit crew   The seven NASCAR team members who put on new tires, fill a car with gas, and do other tasks when the driver pulls in for services during a race

pit road   The area of the racetrack where cars are fixed during a race

pole position   The inside position in the first row of a race's starting grid

rookie   A first-year competitor in a professional sport

sponsors   Companies that pay athletes or teams to use or promote their products

stock car   An automobile made in a factory and available for purchase by the general public

Index